Machines Inside Machines

Using Springs

Wendy Sadler

Raintree

www.raintreepublishers.co.uk
Visit our website to find out more information about **Raintree** books.

To order:
Phone 44 (0) 1865 888112
Send a fax to 44 (0) 1865 314091
Visit the Raintree Bookshop at **www.raintreepublishers.co.uk** to browse our catalogue and order online.

First published in Great Britain by Raintree, Halley Court, Jordan Hill, Oxford OX2 8EJ, part of Harcourt Education.
Raintree is a registered trademark of Harcourt Education Ltd.

Editorial: Melanie Copland and Kate Buckingham
Design: Michelle Lisseter, Victoria Bevan and Bridge Creative Services Ltd
Picture Research: Hannah Taylor
Production: Duncan Gilbert

Originated by Repro Multi Warna
Printed and bound in China by South China Printing Company

10 digit ISBN 1 844 43603 9 (hardback)
13 digit ISBN 978 1 844 43603 3 (hardback)
09 08 07 06 05
10 9 8 7 6 5 4 3 2 1

10 digit ISBN 1 844 43611 X (paperback)
13 digit ISBN 978 1 844 43611 8 (paperback)
10 09 08 07 06
10 9 8 7 6 5 4 3 2 1

British Library Cataloguing in Publication Data
Sadler, Wendy
Using Springs. – (Machines Inside Machines)
621.8'24
A full catalogue record for this book is available from the British Library.

Acknowledgements
The publishers would like to thank the following for permission to reproduce photographs:
Alamy Images (Beateworks Inc) p. **15**; Alamy Images (Ingram Publishing) p. **27**; Alamy Images (Leslie Garland Picture Library) p. **19**; Corbis (George B.Diebold) p. **6**; Corbis (H&S Produktion) p. **21**; Corbis (Kevin Fleming) p. **20**; DK images p. **23**; Getty Images (Botanica) p. **5**; Harcourt Education Ltd (Chrissie Martin) p. **18**; Harcourt Education Ltd (Trevor Clifford) pp. **4**, **17**; Harcourt Education Ltd (Tudor Photography) pp. **7**, **8**, **9**, **13**, **14**, **16**, **22**, **25**, **26**, **28**, **29**; Peter Willis p. **10**; zefa/ masterfile (Gail Mooney) p. **11**; zefa (Satchan) p. **12**.

Cover photograph of springs reproduced with permission of Powerstock/ SuperStock.

Contents

Any words appearing in the text in bold, **like this**, are explained in the glossary.

Machines that use springs

Springs are found in lots of different machines all around you. Springs can be squashed up and stretched out. They can make things pop up or they can hold things in place. We sit on springs in sofas and chairs, and sleep on springs in bed. Cars use springs to make your journey more comfortable. You might even use springs to keep your hair tidy!

Springs on this garden chair make it more comfortable to sit on.

Springs are used in many machines. They can be useful for lots of jobs. They are usually used when you want to make something move or grip. Springs were used in old clocks to keep time. The most important thing about a spring is that it can store **energy**. Energy is the power to make things work. Springs are very simple, but very important.

The spring in these garden cutters helps push the blade apart when you have cut the plant.

What is a spring?

A spring is made of **material** wound into a **cylinder** shape. The shape the spring makes is called a **coil**. A spring needs to be made of **stiff** material to be useful. They are usually made of metal, but they can sometimes be made of very strong plastic as well. Springs are useful because they want to try to stay in their coil shape.

Metal is a stiff material that is good for making springs.

A **simple machine** is something that makes a job easier to do. A spring on its own is not a simple machine. Springs are often used with other simple machines such as wheels, **gears**, and **levers**. When several simple machines are used together we call them **compound machines**. Springs are a very important part of lots of compound machines.

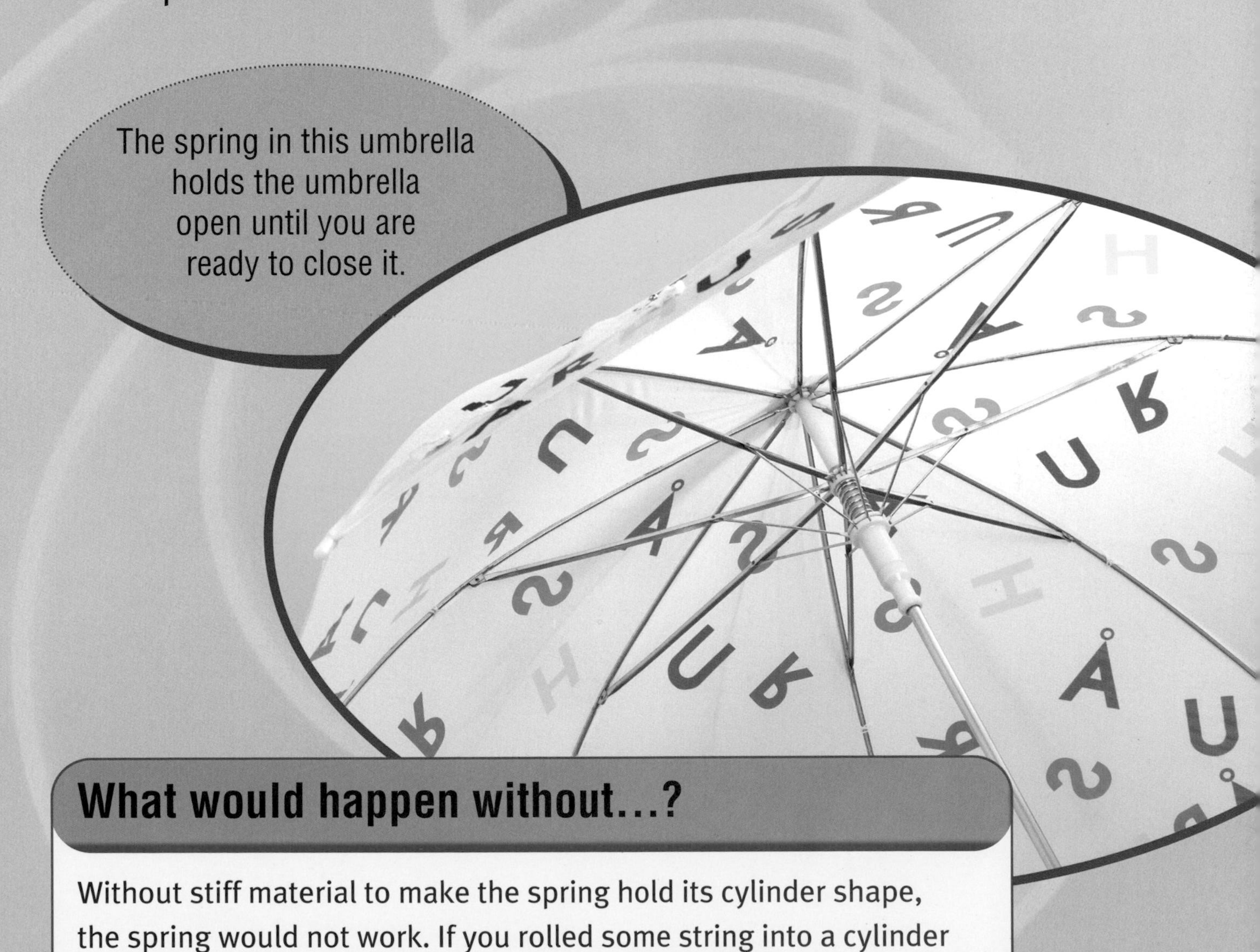

The spring in this umbrella holds the umbrella open until you are ready to close it.

What would happen without...?

Without stiff material to make the spring hold its cylinder shape, the spring would not work. If you rolled some string into a cylinder shape it would not try to hold its shape – it would just unravel.

How does a spring work?

Springs like to stay the same shape as when they are made. All **materials** are made up of tiny pieces called **particles**. The particles inside a spring have strong **forces** between them that hold the material together. When you stretch the spring out, you pull these particles apart. The particles want to get closer together again so the spring pulls back into its original shape.

Some springs are made of strong material and are very difficult to stretch out. Other springs are made of weaker material and can be stretched out easily.

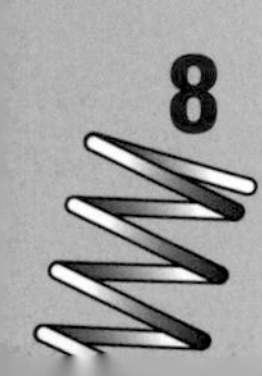

You can also squash a spring by pushing it together. This push makes the particles in the spring get very close together. The forces between them push the particles apart again, to try to return the spring to its usual shape. As soon as you let go, the spring jumps back into shape.

When you close the lid of this jack-in-a-box you squash up the spring. When the lid opens the spring stretches out again and the toy on the end pops up!

Why are springs useful?

Springs are useful because they let us store movement as **energy**. When you push or pull a spring you use your energy to make it change shape. Your energy is now stored in the spring. When you let go, the spring uses the stored energy to move back into its original shape.

When this gate is open the spring stretches out. As soon as you let go of the gate the spring pulls back into shape and brings the gate with it.

The spring in a pinball machine is used to make the ball fly forwards!

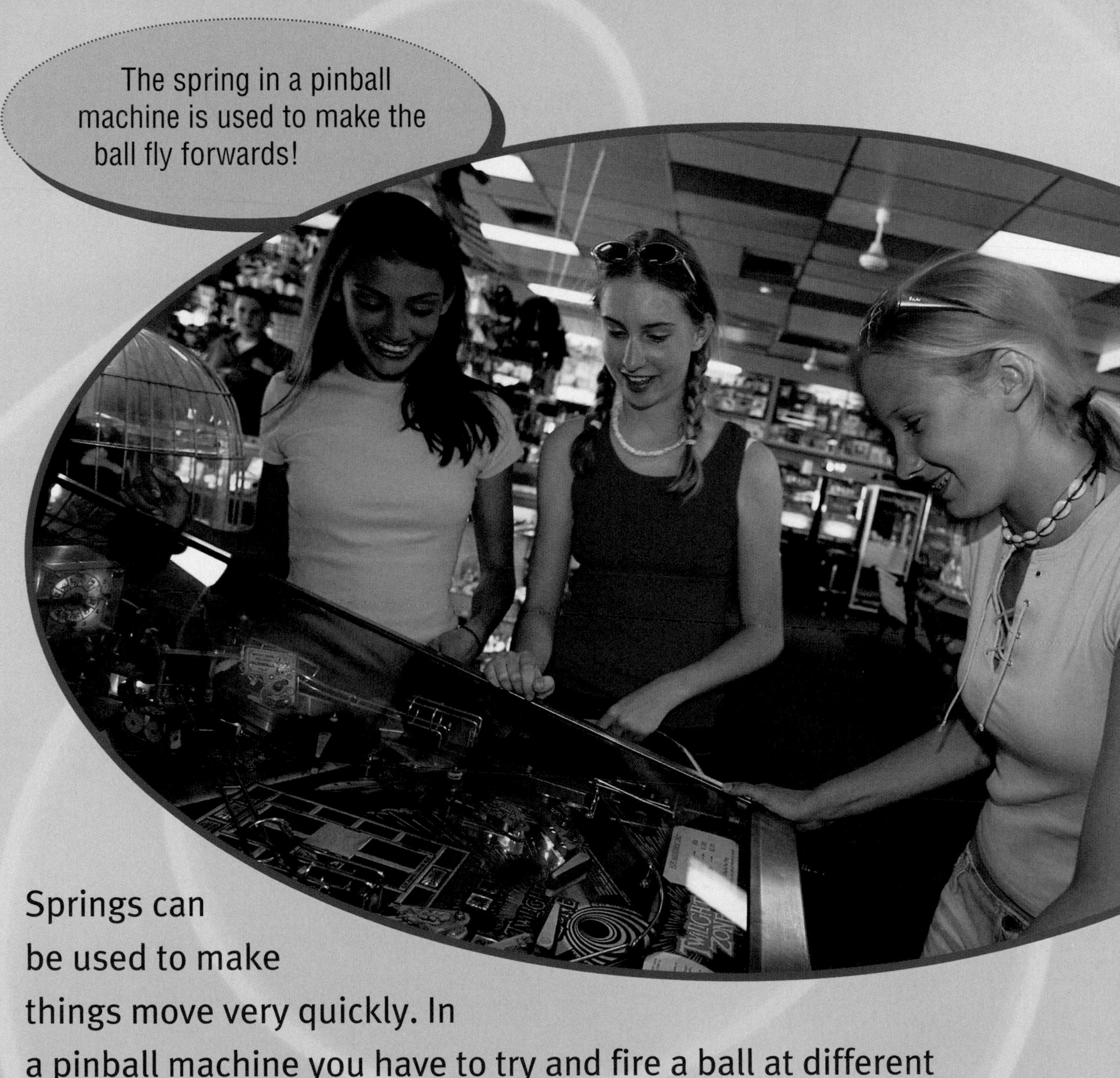

Springs can be used to make things move very quickly. In a pinball machine you have to try and fire a ball at different targets to score points. To launch the ball you pull the spring back so that it is squashed up. The ball sits on the top of the spring. When you let the spring go it jumps back into shape. The spring pushes the ball upwards as it stretches out.

Different types of spring

An **expansion spring** is a spring that is made to be stretched out. The spring tries to pull itself back into shape. When an expansion spring is not stretched out, its **coils** are very close together – sometimes even touching each other.

A chest expander is an example of an expansion spring. This woman is using the strength in her arms to stretch the springs out.

Most springs can only be stretched out up to a certain point. If the spring is made to stretch further than this the **particles** inside will slide past each other. The spring will lose its shape and stay stretched out. Once a spring has been stretched too far it is very difficult to make it go back to its original shape.

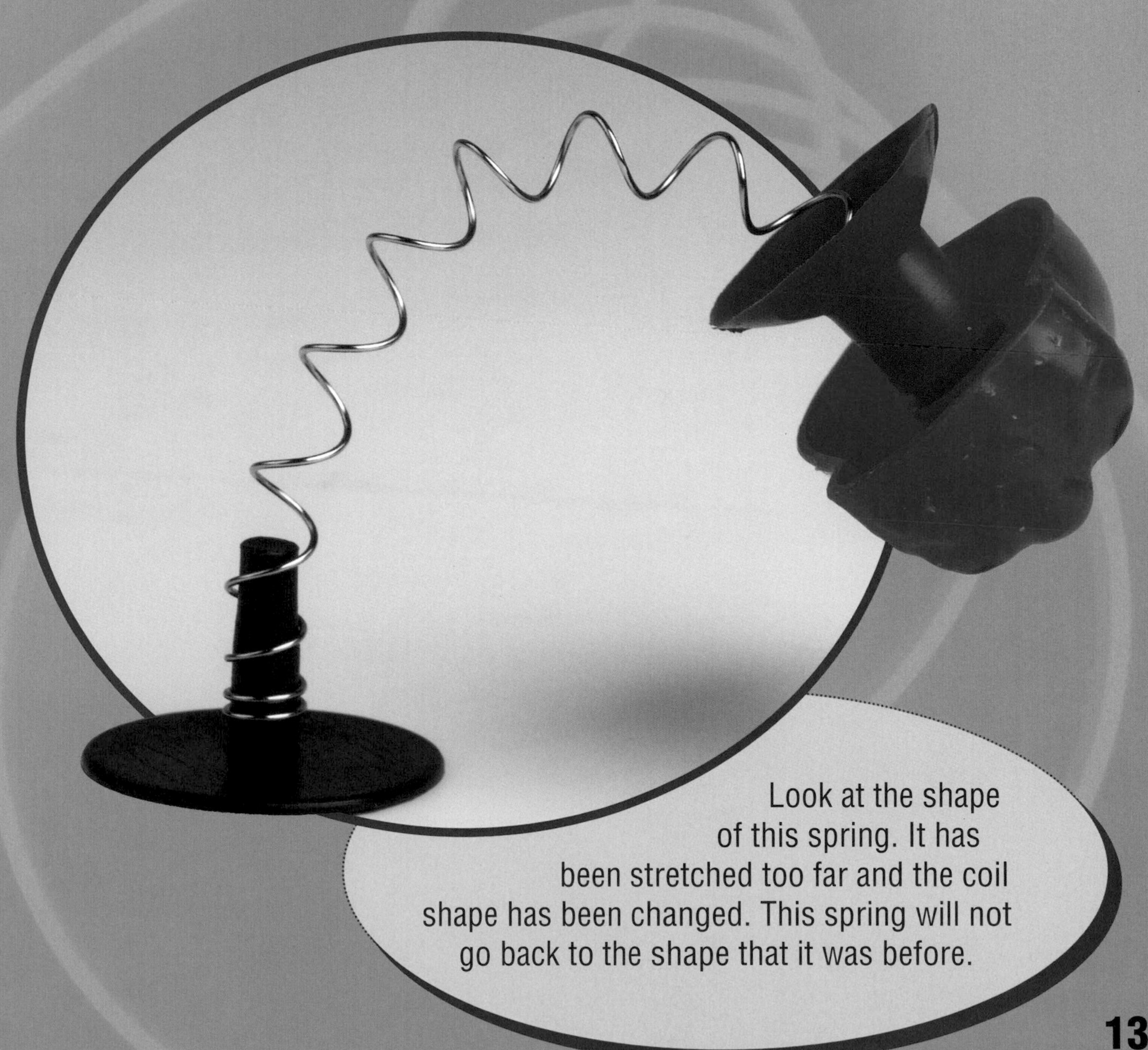

Look at the shape of this spring. It has been stretched too far and the coil shape has been changed. This spring will not go back to the shape that it was before.

Compression springs

A **compression spring** is a spring that is used by squashing it together to store **energy**. A compression spring needs to have some gaps between the **coils** when it is in its usual shape. If there were no gaps between the coils, the coils could not be pushed together.

Once a compression spring has been squashed up so that all the coils are touching, it cannot be pushed any further.

This hole punch uses compression springs. When you punch a hole the springs squash up. When you let go the springs push the hole punch apart again.

Compression springs can be used to grip things. Clothes rails and shower curtain rails can use these springs to hold them up. The spring inside the rail pushes out against the sides of the walls. This keeps the rail from falling down.

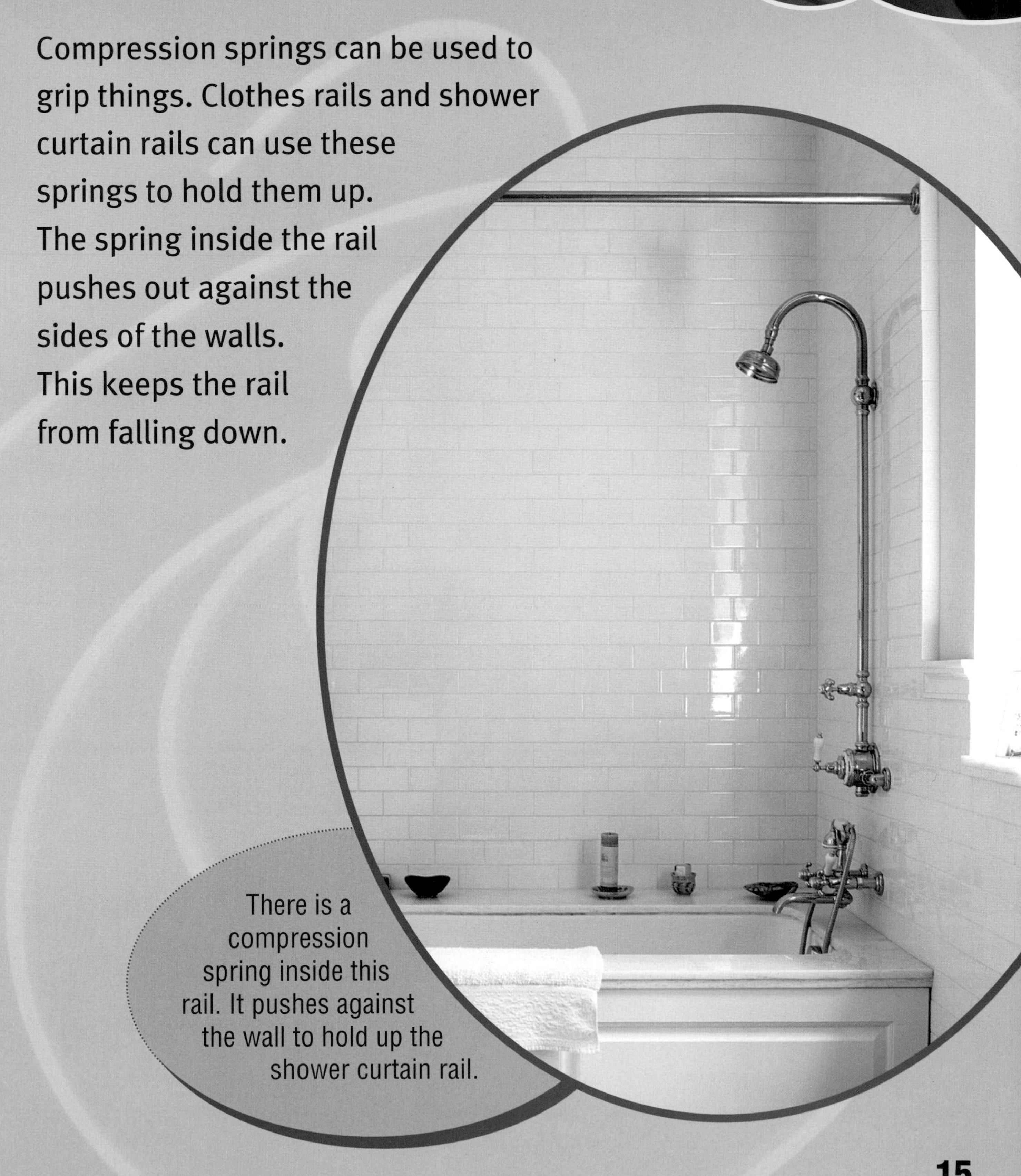

There is a compression spring inside this rail. It pushes against the wall to hold up the shower curtain rail.

Everyday springs

Every time you switch on a light you are probably using a spring without knowing it! The light in your bathroom probably has a string attached to it. When you pull on the string you squash a spring inside the switch. When you let go of the string the spring pushes the switch back upwards. As the switch goes up, the light comes on.

There are springs all around your home – even in the bathroom light switch.

Pens can have springs inside them as well. If a pen does not have a lid, a spring switch can be used to push the writing end in and out of the pen.

Activity

1. Find a pen in your house that has a spring in the end. If you cannot see the spring just try looking for any pen that has a push button on top.
2. Ask an adult to help you take the pen apart and see if you can find the spring inside.

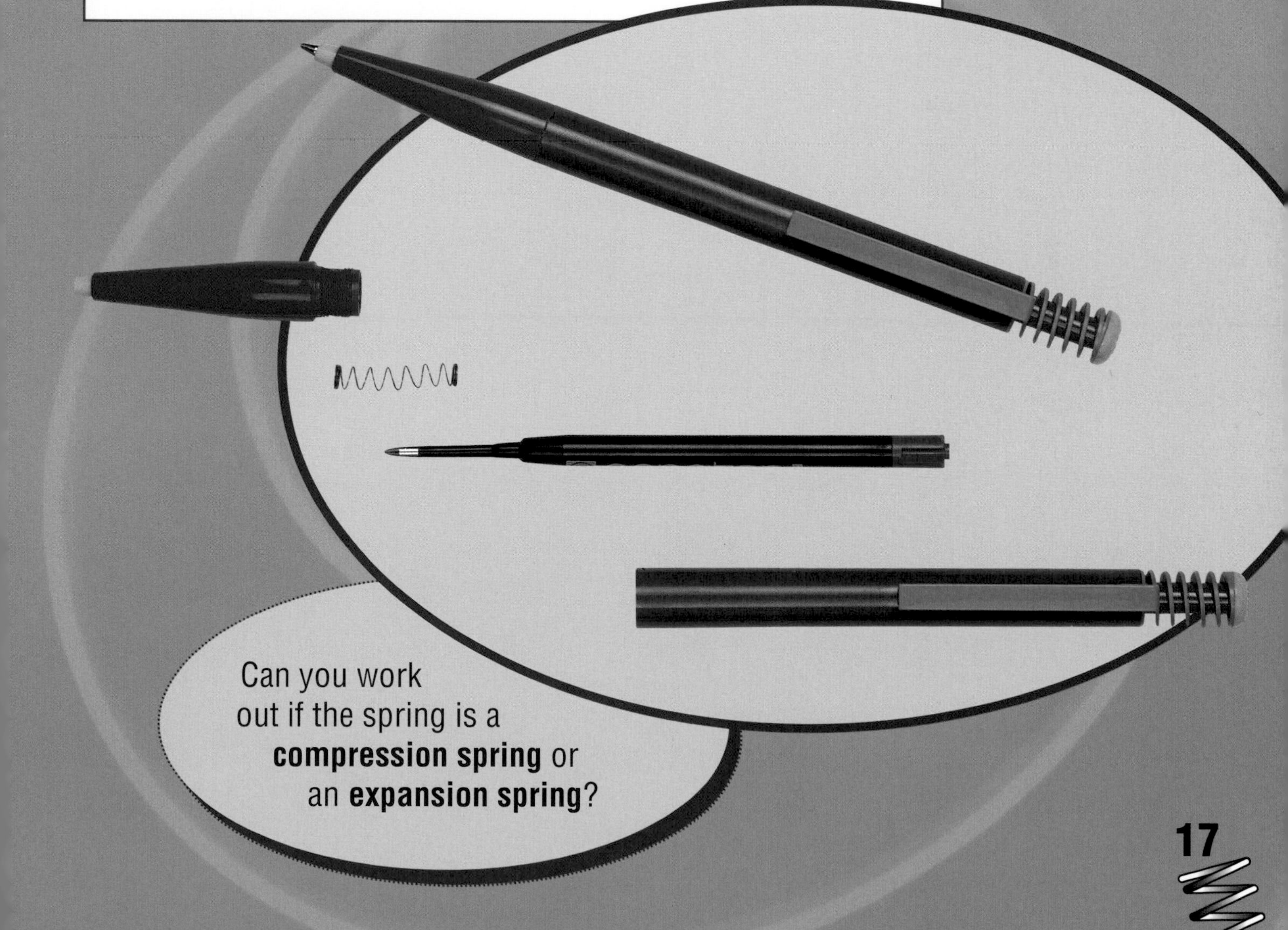

Can you work out if the spring is a **compression spring** or an **expansion spring**?

Springs for a smooth ride

If you look under the seat of a bicycle you may find some springs. They are **compression springs**. When the bicycle wheels go over rocks or stones in the road, the **force** of hitting the stones is used to squash up the springs. Because the force has been used to squash the spring, there is not much force left to reach the person sitting on the seat.

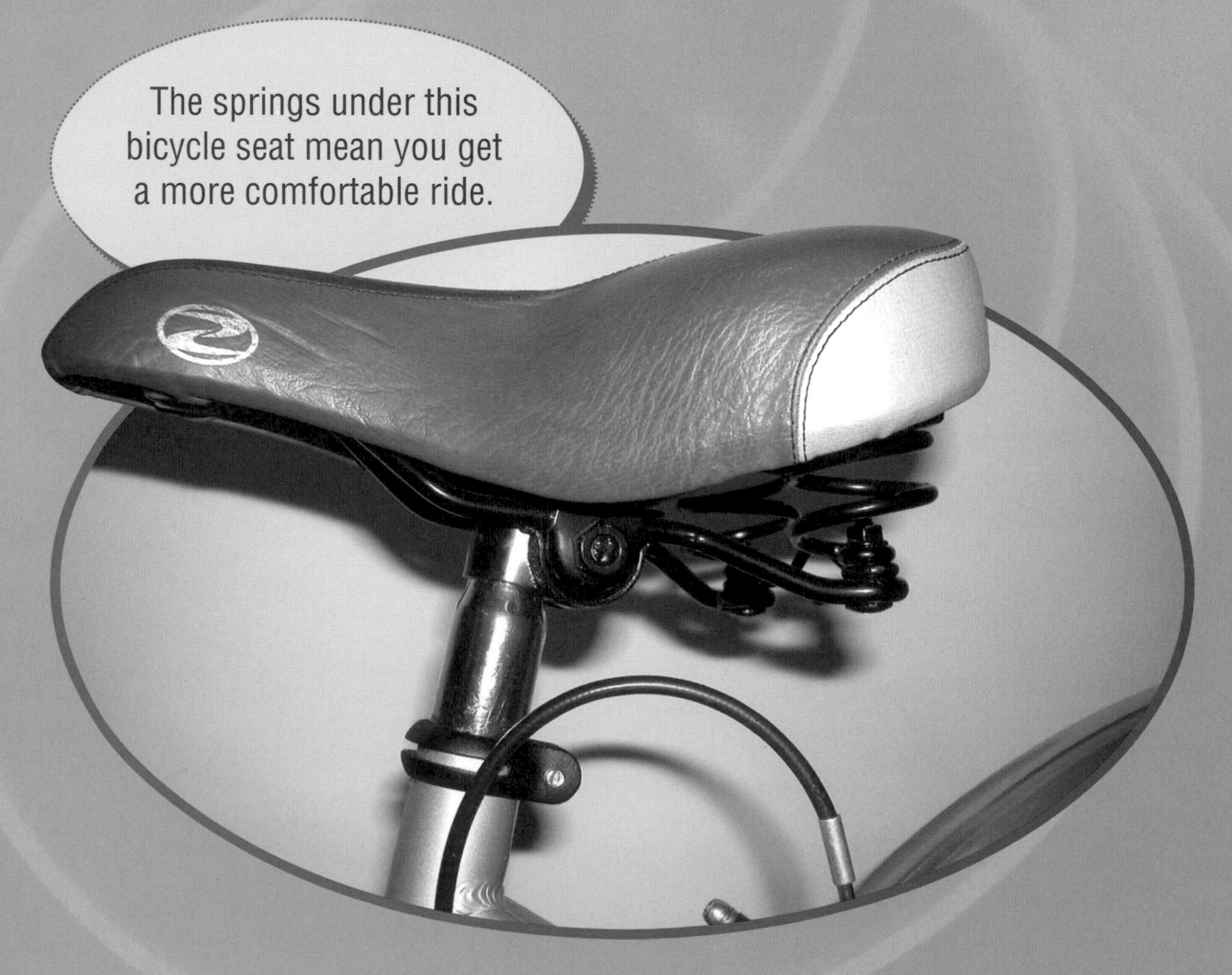

The springs under this bicycle seat mean you get a more comfortable ride.

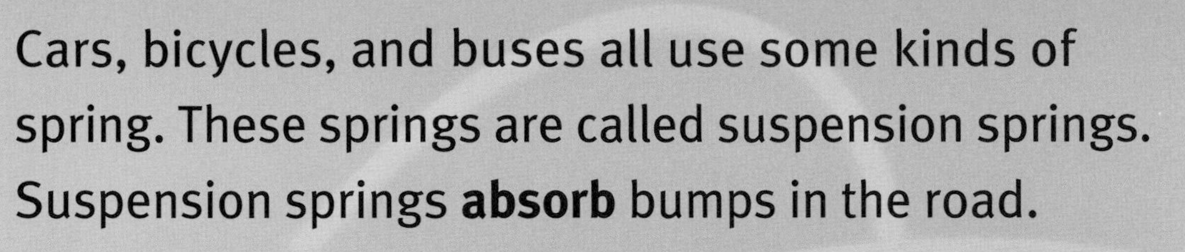

Cars, bicycles, and buses all use some kinds of spring. These springs are called suspension springs. Suspension springs **absorb** bumps in the road. Without springs in vehicles you would feel every stone and dip in the road and your journey could be very painful!

Did you know that springs are used in cars to make your journey more comfortable?

Bouncing with springs

A trampoline uses lots of strong **expansion springs**. The springs join the edge of the trampoline **material** to the side of the trampoline frame. When you bounce, your weight pushes down on the middle of the material. This makes the springs stretch out. All of the springs then want to go back into shape. They start to pull the material back up with them and this makes you lift up and bounce higher!

Without springs, bouncing on a trampoline would not be much fun!

Pogo stick

A pogo stick is a toy with a spring that you can bounce on for fun. A pogo stick has a very strong **compression spring.** As you bounce on the stick, your weight pushes the **coils** of the spring together. The spring stores this **energy** then pushes back into its original shape. As the spring stretches back it pushes the pogo stick upwards so that you can bounce up high.

You need good balance to bounce on a pogo stick.

Interesting springs

Some springs can do surprising things. With a very long **expansion spring** you can make a spring walk downstairs!

To get the spring going it needs to be stretched out.

The spring now wants to pull itself back together again, so it tries to make itself shorter and pulls the back end towards the front.

The force of **gravity** pulls the back end of the spring downwards until it hits the step below. This happens again and again until the spring has reached the bottom of the stairs.

Springs to measure things

A spring can be made longer by pulling on it using a **force**. The distance that a spring will stretch is linked to how much force you use to pull it. This means that we can use springs to measure forces and weights. A big force or a heavy weight will make a spring stretch a long way.

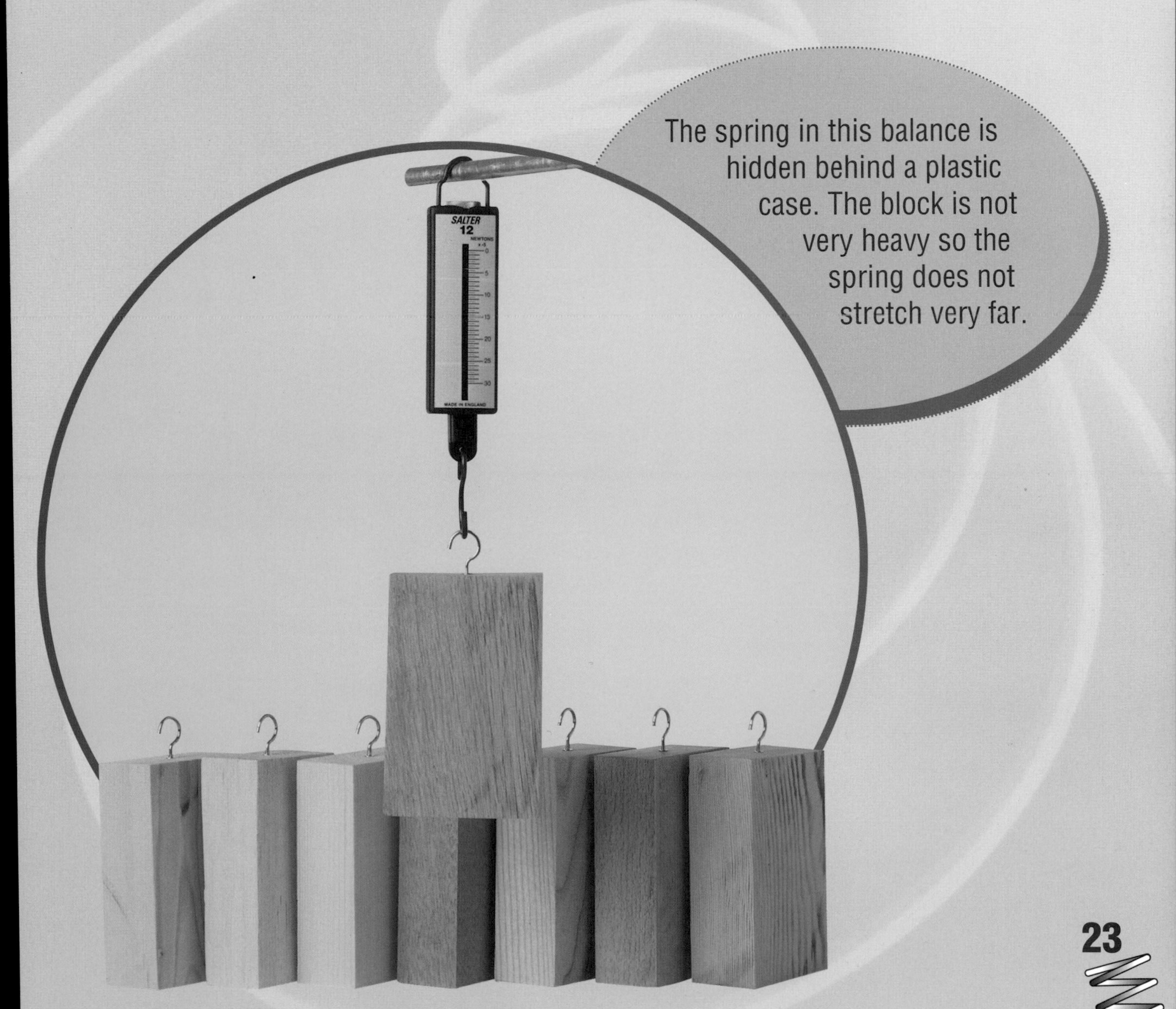

The spring in this balance is hidden behind a plastic case. The block is not very heavy so the spring does not stretch very far.

Springs and levers

The pegs used for hanging clothes out to dry are **compound machines.** They use two **levers** and a spring.

Springs in pegs help them to grip tightly on to your clothes.
spring
jaws

At each end of the spring a small piece of metal sticks out straight. These straight bits are stuck to long pieces of wood or plastic, which act as levers. The levers help you push the spring tighter together than it wants to be. This opens the jaws of the peg. When you let go, the spring pushes back and closes the jaws on to the washing line.

Hair clips

Some hair clips use springs in the same way as clothes pegs. They have teeth that fit together to hold your hair in place. When you press the top of the hair clip, the spring is pushed tightly together and the teeth open up. The spring does not like to be tight so it pushes back and makes the teeth close.

The springs in the hair clip push against the teeth to hold your hair in place.

Sitting on springs

Every day people sit and sleep on lots of springs! Inside sofas, underneath the cushions, there are lots of hidden metal springs that help support your body. These are **compression springs**. When you sit on a sofa you push down on the springs. The springs try to push back to the shape they were before. The pushing of the springs gives support so that you do not sink down into the middle of the sofa.

Springs make your sofa nice and comfortable.

A mattress is the part of your bed that you lie down on. Inside a mattress there are springs held in a frame. They are squashed a little, and push against the mattress **material**. The mattress frame helps to spread out the **force** of each spring so that you cannot feel them pushing against you.

What would happen without...?

If mattresses were just filled with soft material, or foam, they would soon get squashed out of shape. Because the springs push back against the material, they give support and the mattress keeps its shape.

Wind it up...

Old clocks and watches use springs to keep time. A clock is a **compound machine.** It has lots of **simple machines** inside it as well as a special type of spring. The springs used in clocks are called clock springs.

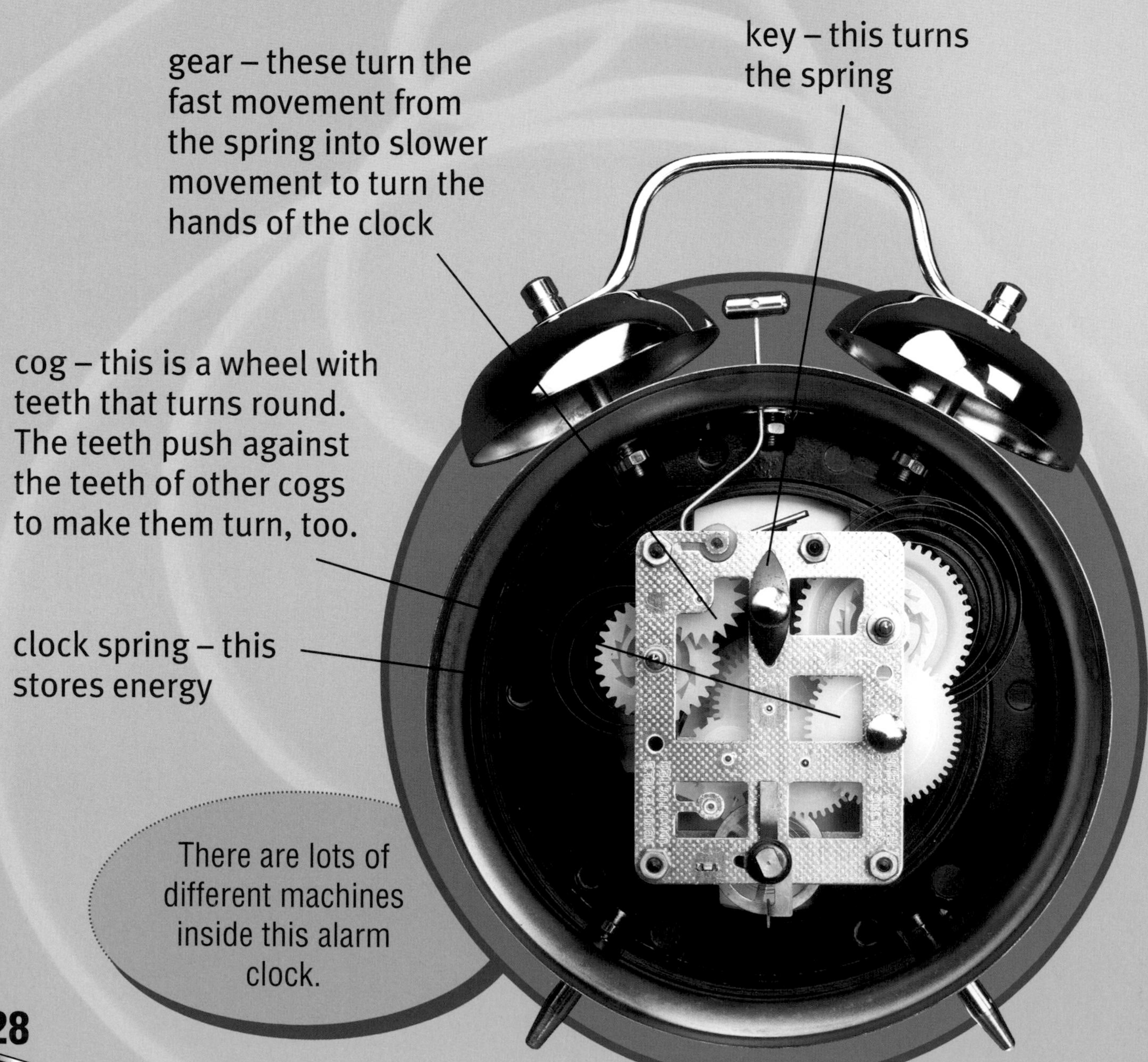
gear – these turn the fast movement from the spring into slower movement to turn the hands of the clock
key – this turns the spring
cog – this is a wheel with teeth that turns round. The teeth push against the teeth of other cogs to make them turn, too.
clock spring – this stores energy

There are lots of different machines inside this alarm clock.

A special key goes into the middle of the clock spring. When the key turns, it tightens the clock spring. The spring stores this **energy** inside the clock. The spring wants to move back to its usual shape. As the spring unwinds, the clock uses **gears** to slow down the movement. Then the hands of the clock move at the right speed and the clock starts ticking.

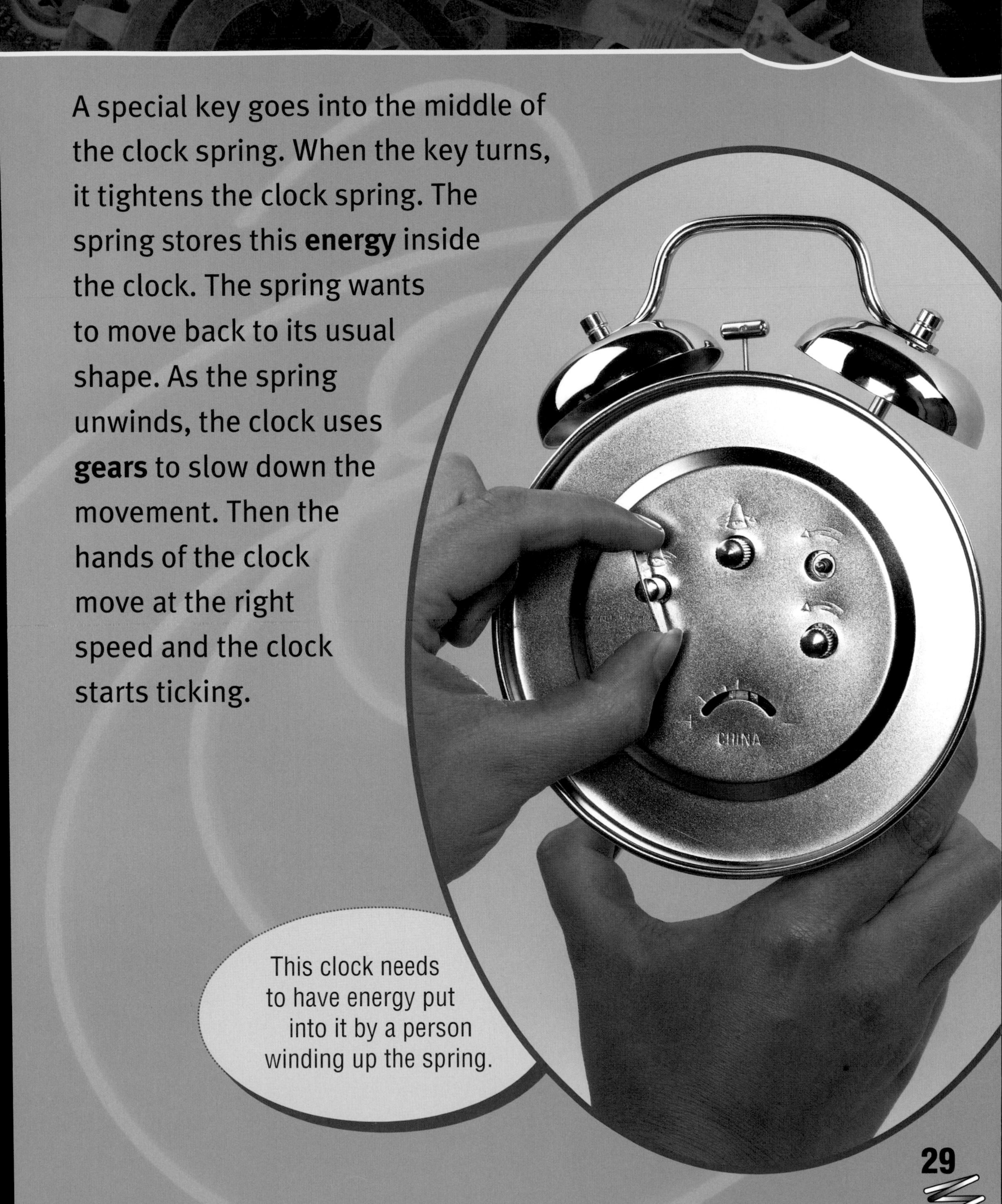

This clock needs to have energy put into it by a person winding up the spring.

Find out for yourself

You can find out about **simple machines** by talking to your teacher or parents. Think about the simple machines you use every day – how do you think they work? Your local library will have books and information about this. You will find the answers to many of your questions in this book, but you can also use other books and the Internet.

Books to read

Science Around Us: Using Machines, Sally Hewitt (Chrysalis Children's Books, 2004)

What do Springs do? David Glover (Heinemann Library, 2001)

Using the Internet

Explore the Internet to find out more about springs. Try using a search engine such as www.yahooligans.com or www.internet4kids.com, and type in keywords such as 'spring', **'coil'**, and **'lever'**.

Glossary

absorb take in

coil length of material wound in circles or rings

compound machine machine that uses two or more simple machines

compression spring spring that is used by squashing it together

cylinder solid shape with straight sides and a rounded end. Drink cans and toilet rolls are cylinder shapes.

energy power to make things work

expansion spring spring that is used by stretching it out

force push or pull. Forces can make things move.

gears wheels with teeth (cogs) working together to change the direction or speed of movement

gravity force that pulls everything towards the ground

lever stiff bar or stick that moves around a fixed point called a fulcrum

material substance that can be used to make things. Wood, brick, plastic and paper are all examples of materials.

particles tiny pieces that all materials are made up of

simple machine something that can change the effort force needed to move something, or change the direction it moves in

stiff something that does not bend easily

Index